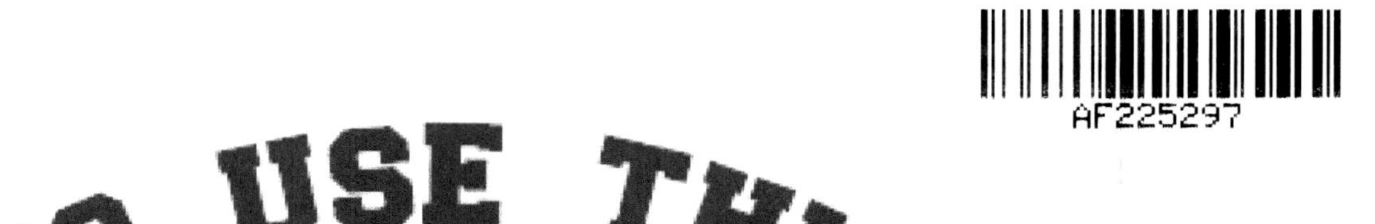

HOW TO USE THIS BOOK

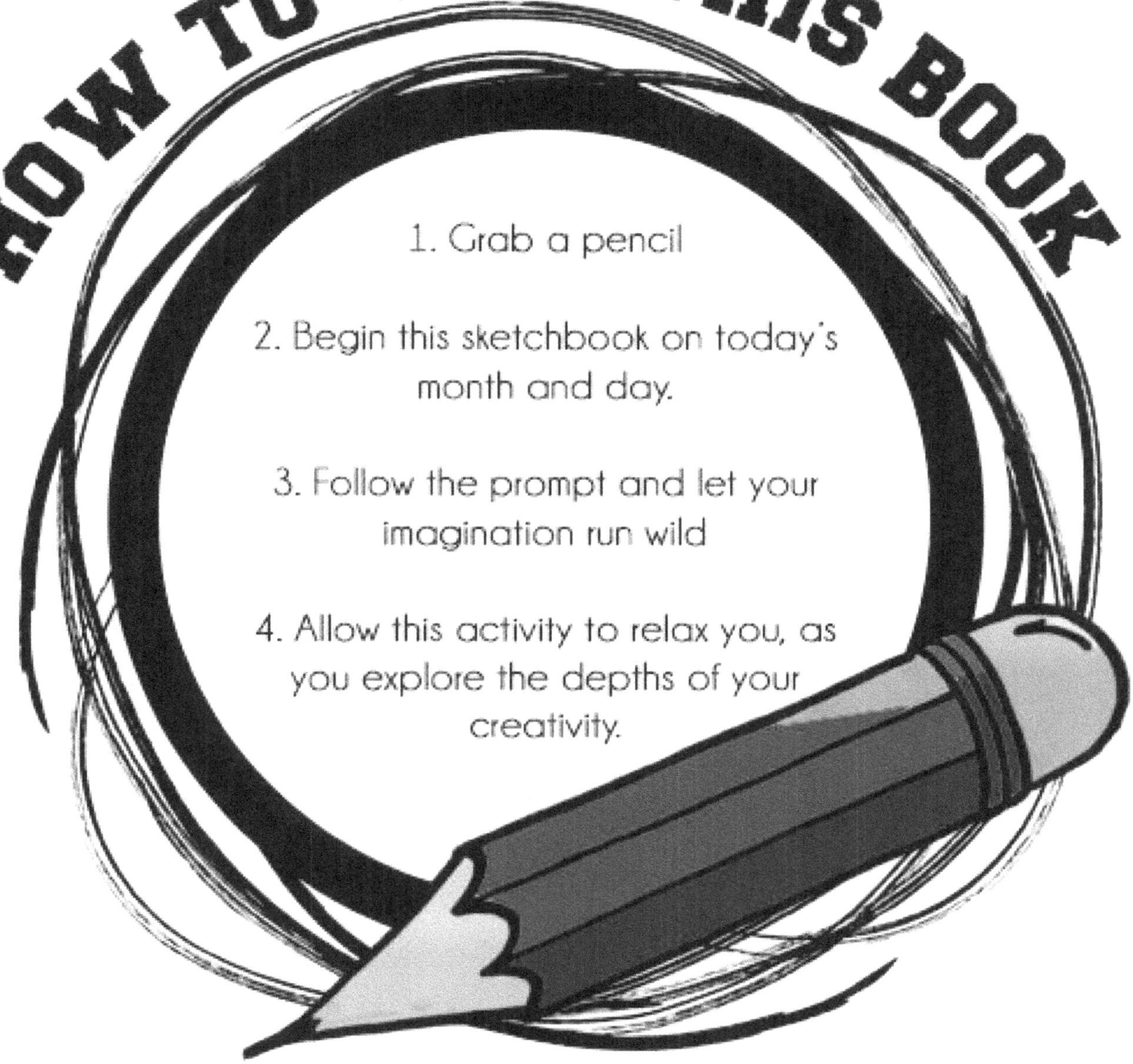

1. Grab a pencil

2. Begin this sketchbook on today's month and day.

3. Follow the prompt and let your imagination run wild

4. Allow this activity to relax you, as you explore the depths of your creativity.

Participate in this challenge to relax daily, or to rapidly improve your drawing skills over the course of a year. To improve at drawing, try your best not to miss any days. Mastery is created out of repetition!

Do: Use photo references (and lots of them). Take risks use techniques you have never tried before.. Think outside the box.

Don't: Stress over a prompt, do what you can. Copy a piece of art you've seen before (inspiration is fine, but you want to develop your own creativity.). Stop imagining and being creative.

JANUARY

1. DRAW A SELF-PORTRAIT

2. WITH YOUR EYES CLOSED DRAW YOUR FAVORITE ANIMAL

3. FILL THIS PAGE WITH EYES IN DIFFERENT POSES (Use reference pictures and photos if needed)

4. AN ELEPHANT

5. FROM OBSERVATION DRAW A TABLECLOTH DRAPED OVER A TABLE (Pay
attention to folds)

6. A CATERPILLAR

7. DO FIVE 1-MINUTE SKETCHES OF PEOPLE YOU HAVE SEEN TODAY (Focus on their gesture or pose)

8. A PET PEEVE

9. BLUEPRINTS FOR AN INVENTION

10. A MYTHICAL CREATURE OR AN ANIMAL THAT DOESN'T EXIST

11. A SOOTHING SOUND

12. WHAT'S IN YOUR BAG?

13. AN ARTICLE OF CLOTHING

14. A ROCKSTAR

15. CAPRICORN ZODIAC SIGN AS A HUMAN OR ANIMAL (Or human or animal like being)

16. A MOUNTAIN VIEW

17. SOMETHING YOU DREAMT RECENTLY

18. A CHILDHOOD MONSTER

19. YOUR FAVORITE SNACK

20. SOMETHING ORANGE (Try going for realism)

21. AN IDIOM (Literalized)

22. A WARM DRINK AS A HOT BABE (Said hot babe can be female, male, or other)

23. A CHARACTER WHO LOOKS VILLAINOUS, BUT IS ACTUALLY QUITE NICE

24. AWAKENING

25. AN EXPLORER

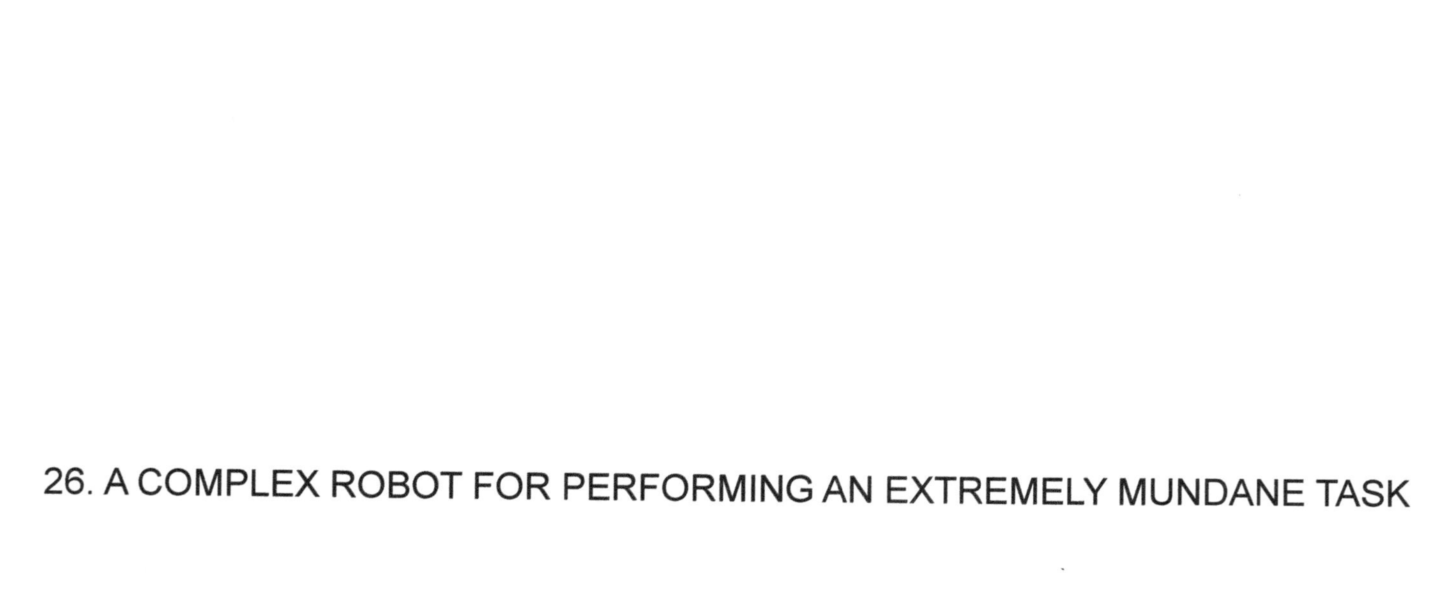

26. A COMPLEX ROBOT FOR PERFORMING AN EXTREMELY MUNDANE TASK

27. AN ICY KING / QUEEN

28. WHAT IS BENEATH THE FROZEN LAKE?

29. A POORLY CAMOUFLAGED PREDATORY ANIMAL

30. TIME TRAVEL / TIME TRAVELER

31. MISFORTUNE

FEBRUARY

1. COLD BREATH

2. A SPIDER

3. FILL THIS PAGE WITH MOUTHS IN DIFFERENT POSES (Use reference pictures and photos if needed)

4. PSYCHEDELIC

5. BIRDS FEEDING PEOPLE

6. WITH YOUR EYES CLOSED DRAW AN ELDERLY PERSON (or animal)

7. AN UNLIKELY BALLERINA

8. AN ALIEN (Violent or peaceful)

9. DO FIVE 1-MINUTE SKETCHES OF PEOPLE YOU HAVE SEEN TODAY (Focus on their gesture or pose)

10. Draw A Violent Storm (Fire, Rain, Wind, etc.)

11. SOMETHING FROM A CHILD'S PERSPECTIVE

12. WHAT IS PEERING AT YOU FROM BEHIND THE CABINET

13. SOMETHING THAT KEEPS YOU WARM

14. A Couple In Love (Cannot be a human couple, but may be humanoid)

15. AQUARIUS ZODIAC SIGN AS A HUMAN OR ANIMAL (Or human or animal-like being)

16. DRAW SOMETHING PURPLE (Use hatching to shade it)

17. DRAW A PIECE OF FABRIC IN MOTION (From observation, or reference)

18. DRAW A FUTURISTIC CITYSCAPE

19. DRAW A PUN, OR PLAY ON WORDS

20. INSANITY

21. DRAW SOMETHING FLUFFY

22. DRAW A MOTORCYCLE

23. DRAW AN INCOMPETENT OFFICER

24. CANDLELIGHT

26. BLURRY

27. EMBRACE

28. A FREEDOM FIGHTER / REBEL

29. TATTOO

MARCH

1. PISCES ZODIAC SIGN AS A HUMAN OR ANIMAL (Or a human or animal-like being)

2. FROM OBSERVATION, DRAW A CLOUDY SKY

3. A PILE OF TOYS

4. DRAW SOMETHING BLUE

5. THE BEST TIME OF DAY

6. SACRIFICE

6. SACRIFICE

7. A METALLIC OBJECT (Pay attention to shading)

8. DISHES THAT HAVEN'T BEEN WASHED YET

9. DO FIVE 1-MINUTE SKETCHES OF PEOPLE YOU HAVE SEEN TODAY (Focus on their gesture or pose)

10. SEAWEED

11. A RED PANDA

12. DRAW AN ALCHEMIST

13. WHAT IS BEHIND THE VEIL

14. FILL THIS PAGE WITH NOSES IN DIFFERENT STYLES AND ANGLES (Use references if needed)

15. A CICADA

16. DO A STUDY DRAW A PATTERNED PIECE OF FOLDED FABRIC

17. A BOWL OF NOODLES (PERSONIFIED)

18. UPSIDE DOWN

19. SOMETHING WEARING A HAT

20. WINGS

21. A MER-CREATURE

22. A BICYCLE

23. A SHAMAN

24. WITH YOUR EYES CLOSED, DRAW YOUR SURROUNDINGS

25. MUDDY

26. CAPTIVE

27. CRYSTALS

28. SOMETHING HATCHING FROM AN EGG

29. DREAMY

30. A SUPERHERO WITH POWERS YOU WOULD NEVER WANT

31. AN ANGRY CROWD

APRIL

1. DANCERS

2. A CENTIPEDE

3. FILL THIS PAGE WITH HUMAN SKULLS (Focus on accuracy, shading and angles. Use references if needed)

4. A FAST CAR

5. SWOLLEN

6. ARIES ZODIAC SIGN AS A HUMAN OR ANIMAL (or a human or animal-like being)

7. RAINY

8. DO FIVE 1-MINUTE SKETCHES OF PEOPLE YOU HAVE SEEN TODAY (Focus on their gesture or pose)

9. RUNNING SHOES

10. DRAW A CREATURE WITH HORNS

11. A SOLDIER

12. SCISSORS

13. HIBISCUS

14. DEEP DISCUSSION

15. DRENCHED

16. INFERNO

18. A CLEARING IN A FOREST

19. GATES

20. DRAW PLAYERS OF A SPORT YOU MADE UP

22. WITH YOUR EYES CLOSED, DRAW SOMETHING RED

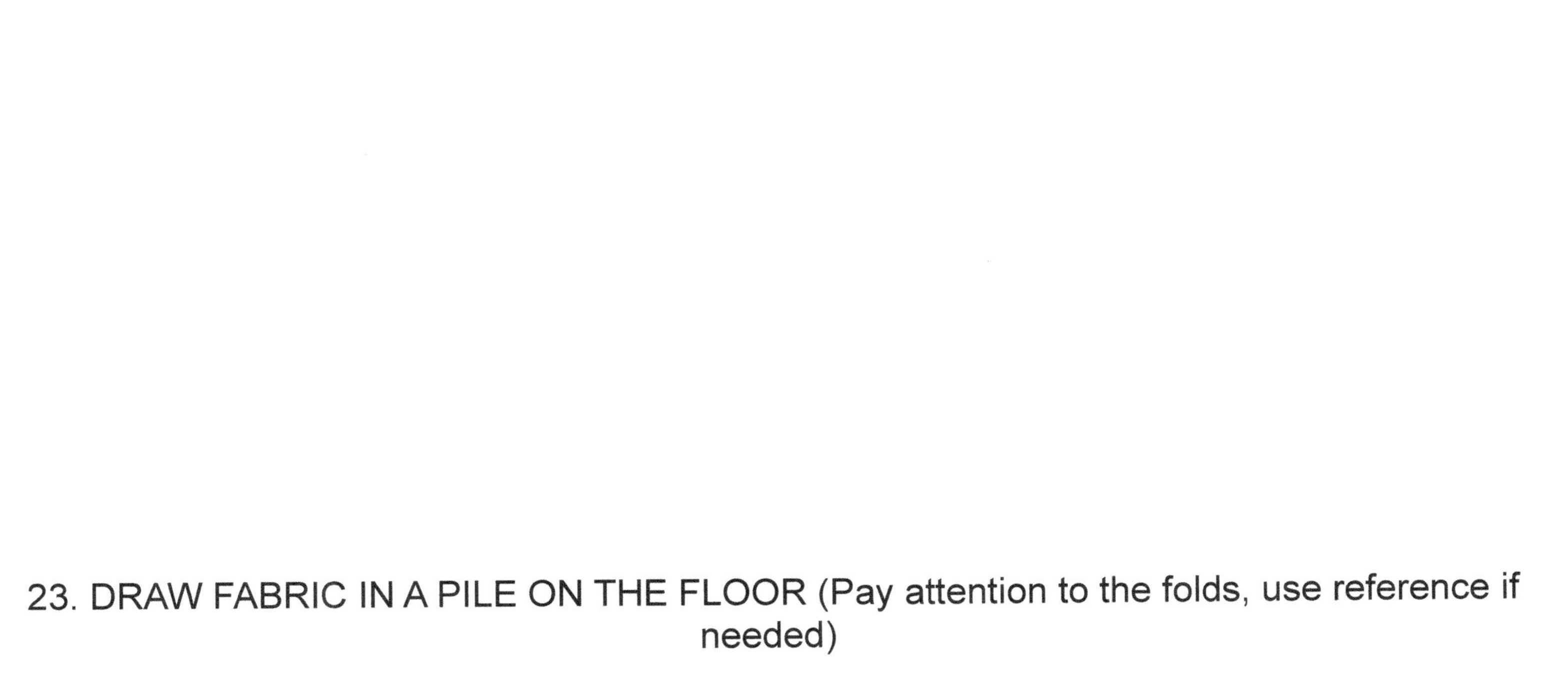

23. DRAW FABRIC IN A PILE ON THE FLOOR (Pay attention to the folds, use reference if needed)

24. PICK A SONG TITLE, AND DRAW IT

26. HUNTER

27. A BOOK CHARACTER (No film adaptations)

28. WHAT JUST FLEW BY?

29. SEDUCTION

30. SURVIVAL

MAY

1.   A BARD

2. A BUMBLEBEE

3. A ROSE

4. UNDERGROUND

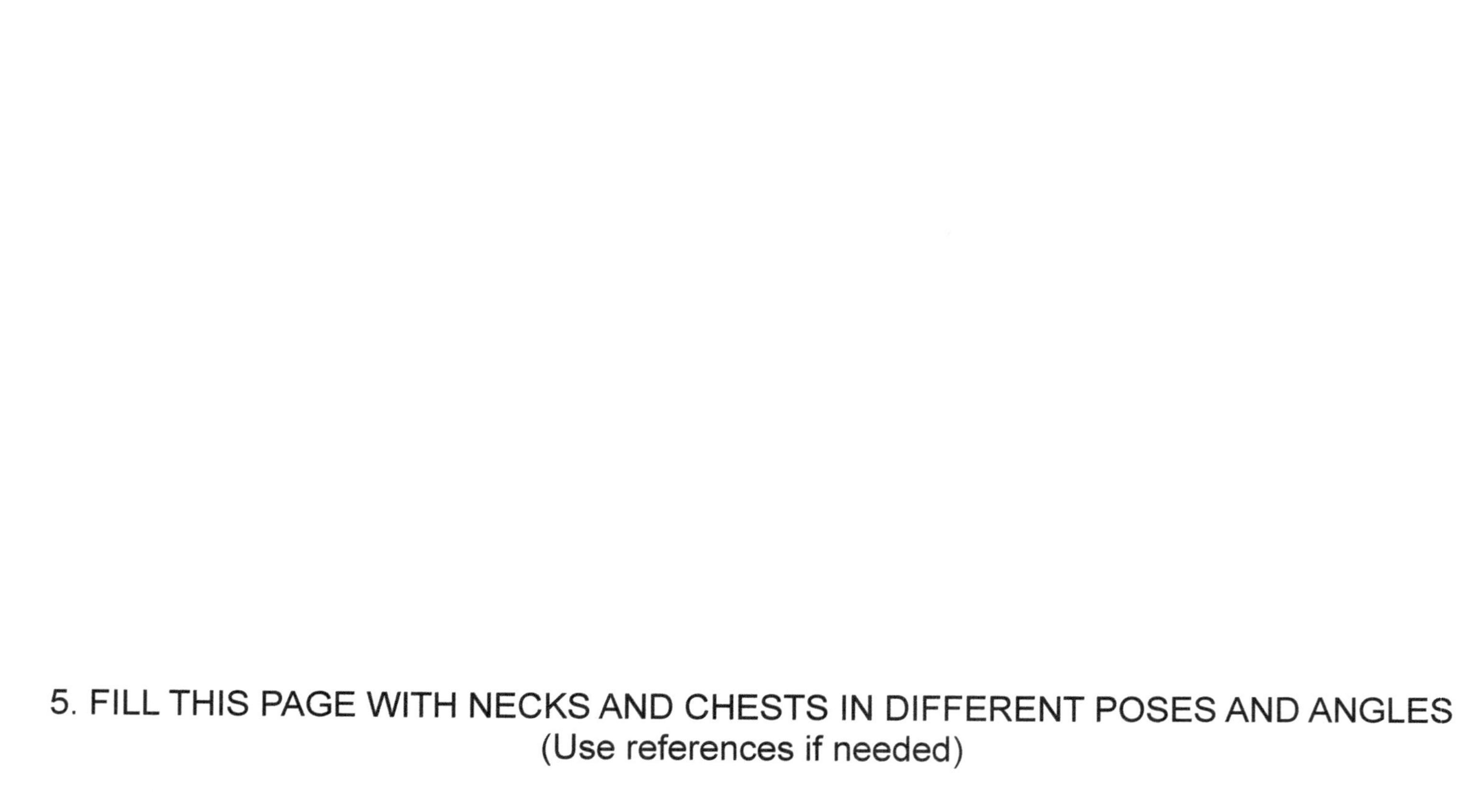

5. FILL THIS PAGE WITH NECKS AND CHESTS IN DIFFERENT POSES AND ANGLES
(Use references if needed)

7. FEATHERY

8. MELODIC LAUGHTER

9. FILL THIS PAGE WITH EARS, DIFFERENT STYLES AND ANGLES (Use references if needed)

11. A CLOVEN CREATURE

13. A HOT AIR BALLOON

14. TAURUS ZODIAC SIGN AS A HUMAN OR ANIMAL (Or human or animal-like being)

15. SLOWLY, SLOWLY

16. WITH YOUR EYES CLOSED, DRAW A GROUP OF TOADSTOOLS

17. A PLANT, MAKE IT DEADLY

19. UNDERWEAR

20. WHAT IS THAT GUY EATING?

21. DO FIVE 1-MINUTE SKETCHES OF PEOPLE YOU HAVE SEEN TODAY (Focus on their gesture or pose)

22. DARK MATTER

23. CHOOSE A POEM TO READ, DRAW WHAT COMES TO MIND

24. EXOTIC

25. PLAYFUL

26. SOMETHING YELLOW

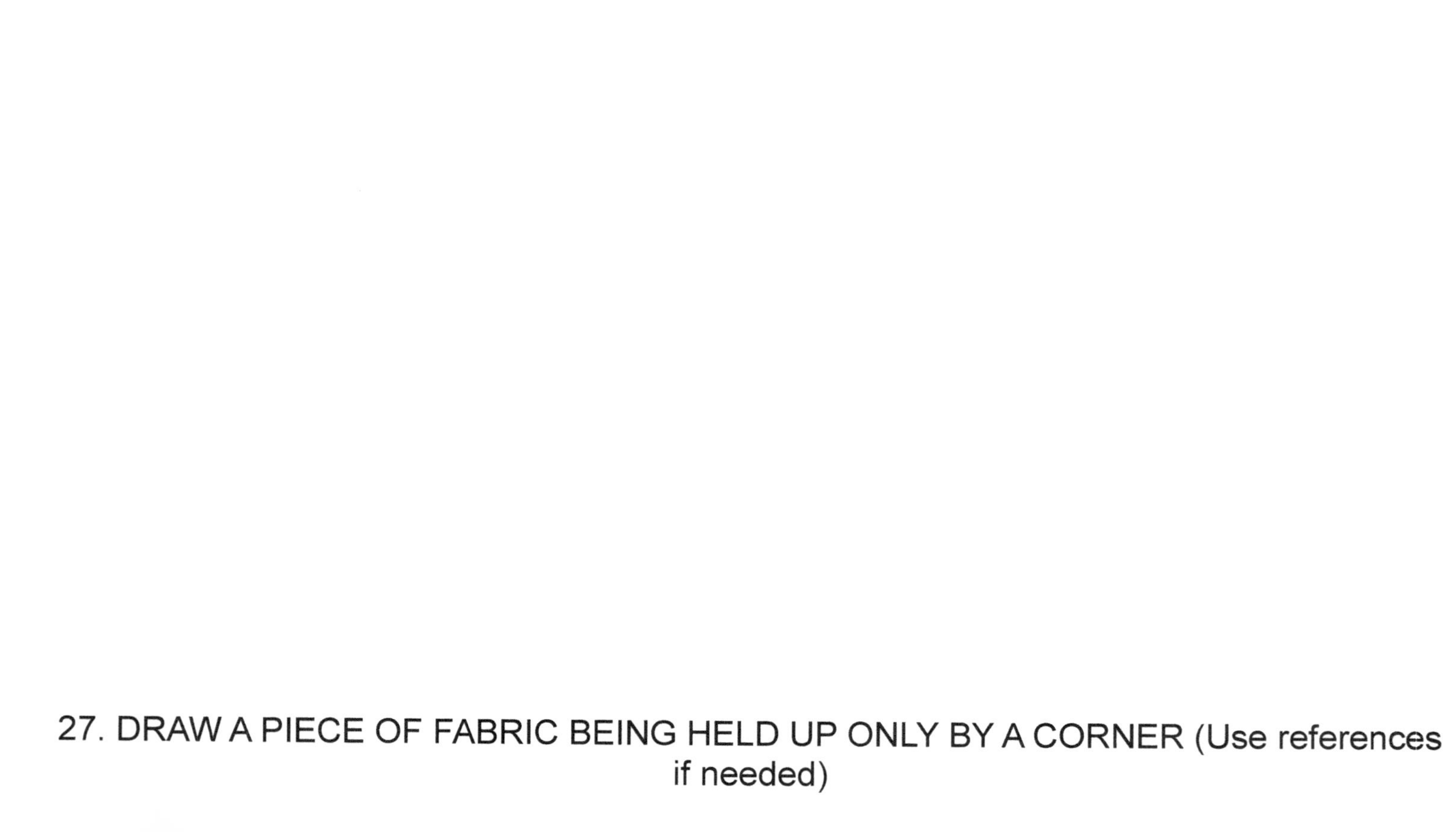

27. DRAW A PIECE OF FABRIC BEING HELD UP ONLY BY A CORNER (Use references if needed)

28. ETHEREAL

29. A DREADFUL SMILE

30. A JESTER, TRICKSTER, OR CLOWN

31. POTS AND PANS

JUNE

1. EXTREME CLOSE-UP

2. DRAW FABRIC DRAPED OVER A HUMAN FORM (Pay attention to folds, use references if needed)

3. GIGANTIC

4. A BEETLE

5. WOODLANDS

6. A LOAF OR BREAD

7. FILL THIS PAGE WITH HANDS IN DIFFERENT POSES (Use references if needed)

8. CHARMED

9.CHERRY BLOSSOMS

10. SHADOW AND LIGHT INTERPLAY

11. A FARMER

13. ROLLERSKATES

14. DO FIVE 1-MINUTE SKETCHES OF PEOPLE YOU HAVE SEEN TODAY (Focus on
their gesture or poses)

16. WHAT KEEPS POKING YOU?

17. MOONLIGHT

18. GROTESQUE AND BEAUTIFUL

19. GEMINI ZODIAC SIGN AS A HUMAN OR ANIMAL (OR human or animal-like being)

20. TONGUE

21. CHOOSE A QUOTE, DRAW IT

22. A COUCH

23. WITH YOUR EYES CLOSED, DRAW A COSMIC BEING

24. RECOIL

25. KEYS

26. PINCH

27. BEARD AND / OR MOUSTACHE

29. VOLUPTUOUS

30. BUBBLES

JULY

1. THE WORST BAKER EVER

2. COMFORTED

3. FOLIAGE

4. A BEACH

6. A DRAGONFLY

7. DRAW CANCER ZODIAC SIGN AS A HUMAN OR ANIMAL (Or human or animal-like being)

8. SOMETHING PINK

9. A TULIP

10. BONFIRE / CAMPFIRE

11. A PREHISTORIC CREATURE (Real or not)

12. BATTLE ARMOR

13. COILED SERPENT

14. TSUNAMI

15. LEANING

16. WHERE IS THAT SMELL COMING FROM?

17. A TUX / SUIT

18. A JET

19. DO FIVE 1-MINUTE SKETCHES OF PEOPLE YOU HAVE SEEN TODAY (Focus on their gesture and pose)

20. LIGHTNING AND PLASMA

21. DRAW A NON-HUMAN FAMILY PORTRAIT

22. A PAGE

23. PSYCHIC

24. SLEEP

25. QUEST

26. WITH YOUR EYES CLOSED, DRAW SOMETHING SLIMY

27. FILL THIS PAGE TORSOS IN DIFFERENT POSITIONS AND POSES (Use references if needed)

28. SECRET

29. PATIENCE

30. ANGELIC

31. HERO

AUGUST

1. SPELLCRAFT

31. SUNFLOWER

4. DRAW SOMEONE IN A DRESS (Focus on the folds, pleats or ruffles in the fabric)

5. SOMETHING GRAY

6. DRAW LEO ZODIAC SIGN AS A HUMAN OR ANIMAL (Or human or animal-like being)

7. SOMBER

8. WITH YOUR EYES CLOSED, DRAW A MASK

9. BAMBOO

10. CLAWS

11. REGAL

12. SAVANNAH

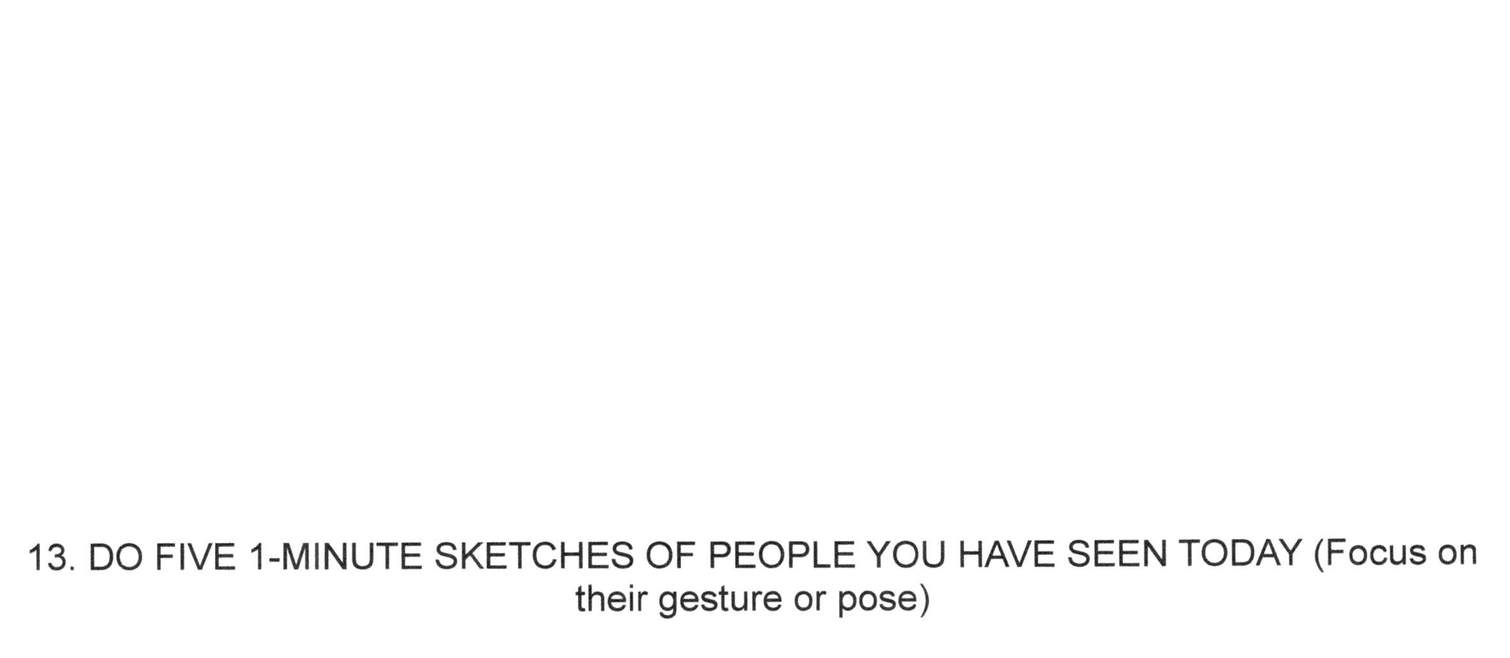

13. DO FIVE 1-MINUTE SKETCHES OF PEOPLE YOU HAVE SEEN TODAY (Focus on their gesture or pose)

14. TEARS

15. OBSCURED

16. EXTRAVAGANCE

17. A TANK

18. ANTLERS

19. AN ACROBAT

20. BABY

21. POCKETS

22. FELINE

23. FILL THIS PAGE WITH THE HUMAN SKELETON (Focus on accuracy, poses and position)

24. Lies

25. WITCHY

26. DRAW SOMETHING FROM A DROWSY PERSON'S POV

27. CROSSING A BRIDGE

28. LIMBO

29. DRAW WHAT SOMEONE WOULD SEE PEERING INTO A KEYHOLE

30. ASHES

31. AN ORCHID

SEPTEMBER

1. A CAVE

2. SURGERY

3. PRAYING MANTIS

4. HARVEST

5. GENIUS

6. DO FIVE 1-MINUTE SKETCHES OF PEOPLE YOU HAVE SEEN TODAY (Focus on their gesture and pose)

7. STERILE

8. PRISTINE

9. VIRGO ZODIAC SIGN AS A HUMAN OR ANIMAL (Or human or animal-like being)

10. SOMETHING GREEN

11. SMOKY

12. SCARECROW

13. NARCISSUS (Flower)

14. DRAW A WET PIECE OF FABRIC (Use references if needed)

15. WHERE IS THAT SOUND COMING FROM?

16. MAGNIFIED

17. A BOAT

18. A CREEK

19. DUST

20. FILL THIS PAGE WITH ARMS IN DIFFERENT POSES AND ANGLES (Use references if needed)

21. MEDICINE MAN/ WOMAN

22. HUNGER

23. BATHTUB

24. A MOLLUSK

25. JUMP

26. DRAW SOMETHING SHOCKING FROM THE VIEW OF YOUR BEDROOM WINDOW

27. IF YOUR FAVORITE ANIMAL COULD DRAW, WHAT WOULD IT DRAW, AND HOW
WOULD IT PICTURES LOOK

28. MIRROR IMAGE

29. WITH YOUR EYES CLOSED DRAW A HUGE BOWL OF ICE-CREAM

30. SOMETHING FROM A DOG'S EYE VIEW

OCTOBER

1. A PARADE, WHAT OR WHO IS IT FOR?

2. DANGER

3. SURRENDER

4. INEBRIATION

5. AN ANT

6. CHANGE THE SCALE OF TWO OBJECTS, AND DRAW THEM BESIDE EACH OTHER

7. CASANOVA

8. VINES

9. DRAW SOMETHING WITH YOUR NON-DOMINANT HAND

10. A TRAIN

11. DRAW SOMEONE IN SOAKED CLOTHING (Focus on how the fabric clings and gathers)

12. LIBRA ZODIAC SIGN AS A HUMAN OR ANIMAL (Or human or animal-like being)

13. FUNKY

14. DO FIVE 1-MINUTE SKETCHES OF PEOPLE YOU HAVE SEEN TODAY (Focus on
their pose and gesture)

15. A RAVEN

16. FOG

17. AWAKEN

18. ASSASSIN

19. HOW IN THE WORLD DID THAT COUPLE GET TOGETHER?

21. FILL THIS PAGE WITH LEGS IN DIFFERENT POSES AND ANGLES (Use references if needed)

22. FANGS

24. SOMETHING WHITE

25. TRANSFORMATION

26. LIE ON THE GROUND, AND DRAW WHAT YOU SEE

27. DRAW A HALLWAY (1 POINT PERSPECTIVE)

28. WITH YOUR EYES CLOSED DRAW A VAMPIRE

29. A DESERT

30. WILL-O-WISP

31. SPIRIT OF HALLOWEEN

NOVEMBER

1. DOUGHNUT

2. SWIRLING

3. FROST

4. RITUAL

5. SOMETHING BROWN

6. DO FIVE 1-MINUTE SKETCHES OF PEOPLE YOU HAVE SEEN TODAY (Focus on their gesture or pose)

7. WITH YOUR EYES CLOSED DRAW SOMETHING POISONOUS

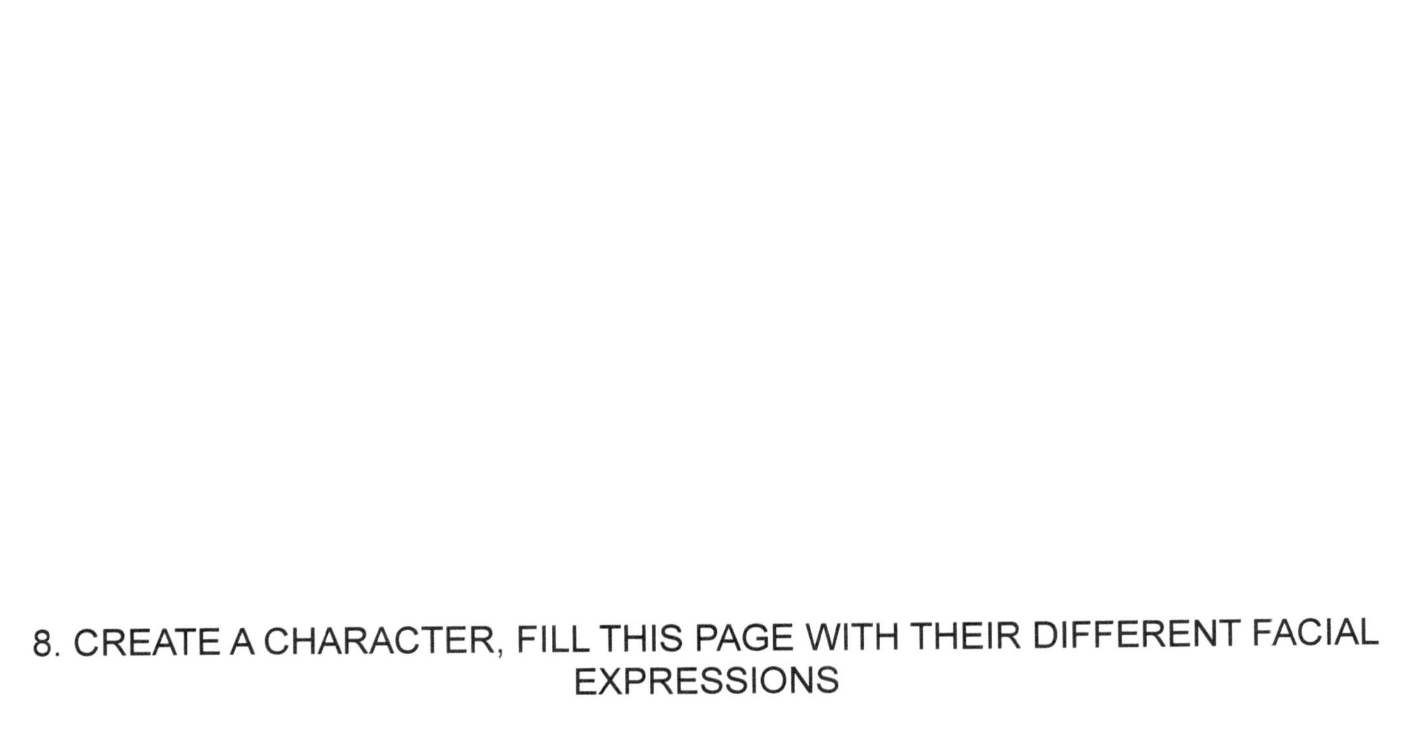

8. CREATE A CHARACTER, FILL THIS PAGE WITH THEIR DIFFERENT FACIAL EXPRESSIONS

9. A MARANTAS

10. FIREWORKS

11. TAPESTRY

12. DRAW A PIECE OF TATTERED FABRIC (Use references if needed)

13. AN OWL

14. YAWN

15. SCORPIO ZODIAC SIGN AS A HUMAN OR ANIMAL (Or human or animal-like being)

16. IMPALED

18. HIDDEN

19. A MOTH

20. KISS

21. WHAT DID YOU JUST STEP ON?

22. DRAW A CHARACTER, THEN DRAW THEM IN A SURREAL STYLE

23. LITHE

24. STRANGER ON THE THRESHOLD

25. A BLACKSMITH

26. SPACE

27. A PERSON BY THE LIGHT OF A COMPUTER, TV, OR CELLPHONE SCREEN

28. PHOENIX

29. MITTENS

30. LIMP

DECEMBER

1. HIBERNATION

2. A WASP

3. DRIPPING

4. A CHIEF

5. BLUSTERY

6. Stumbling

7. A HAWK

8. DO FIVE 1-MINUTE SKETCHES OF PEOPLE YOU HAVE SEEN TODAY (Focus on their gesture and pose)

9. DRAW A TOWN ON ANOTHER PLANET

10. DEPTHS

11. SPIKY AND SOFT

12. DRAW A WALL AND ACCOMPANYING GRAFFITI

13. SNOW GLOBE

14. ASTRAL

15. HOPE

16. BLIZZARD

17. SAGITTARIUS ZODIAC SIGN AS A HUMAN OR ANIMAL (Or human or animal-like being)

18. DRAW SOMEONE IN OLD WORLD ATTIRE (VICTORIAN, KEMETIC, ANCIENT GREEK ETC.)

19. DRAW SOMEONE YOU KNOW AS AN ANIMAL

20. RHYTHM

21. A DANGEROUS PET

22. WITH YOUR EYES CLOSED, DRAW SOMETHING SCALY

24. TWO UNLIKELY FRIENDS

25. STARS

27. AN OBJECT LIT BY A SOURCE (Flashlight, candlelight, spotlight)

28. ICICLES

30. SUNBEAM

31. DRAW WHATEVER YOU WANT!

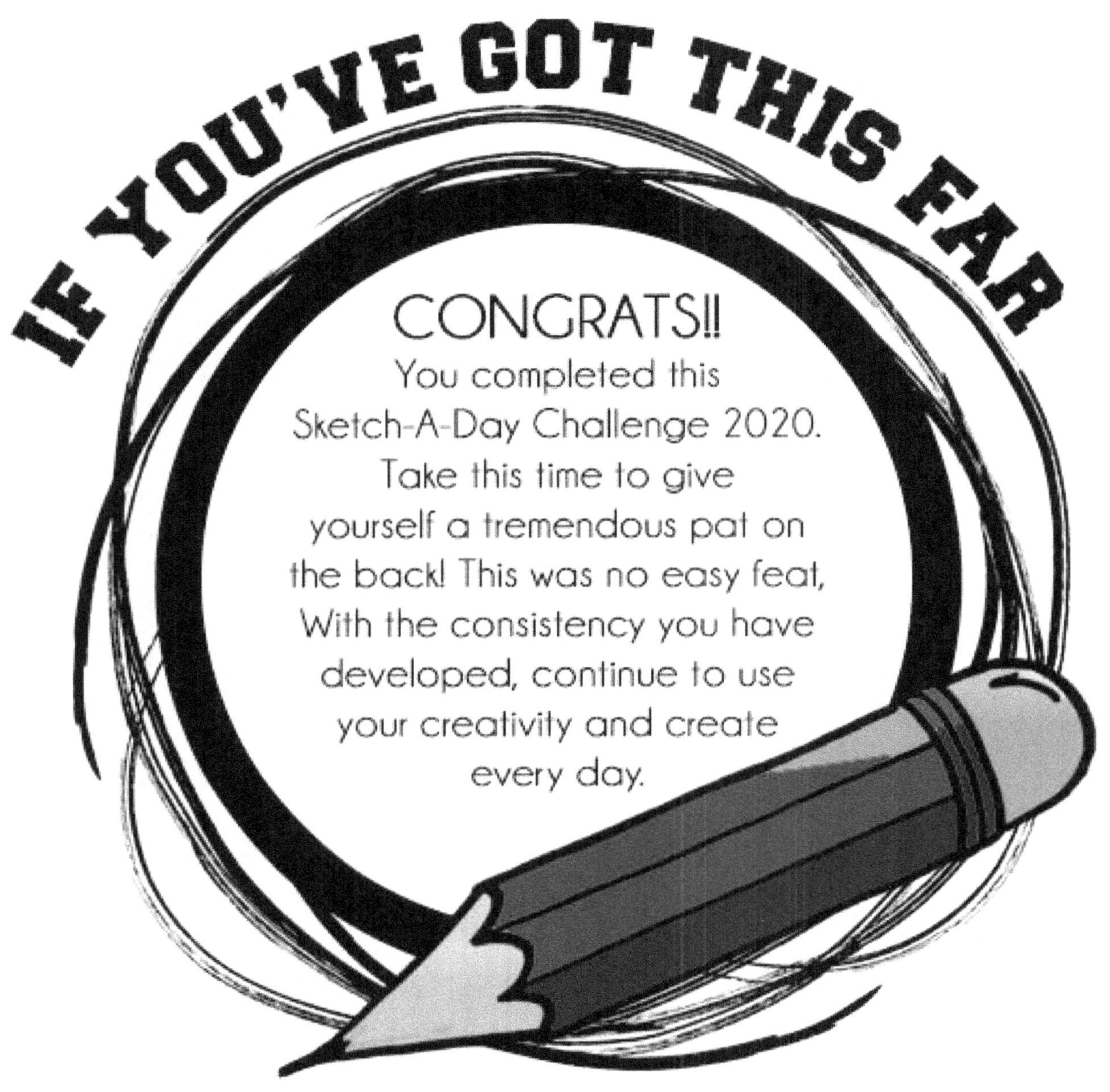

WE HOPE THAT THIS BOOK HELPED TO STIR YOUR IMAGINATION, IMPROVE YOUR DRAWING AND OBSERVATION SKILLS, AND RELAX INTO A HOBBY YOU LOVE!

BUT DON'T STOP HERE, CONTINUE DRAWING, KEEP CREATING WELL INTO 2021 AND BEYOND!